Miracles and Healings

Renewing the Mind Series

By

Marjorie Lou

Unless otherwise indicated, all Scripture quotations are taken from the
Holy Bible, English Standard Version® (ESV®),
copyright © 2001by Crossway, a publishing ministry of
Good News Publishers. Used by permission. All rights reserved.

Miracles and Healings
Renewing the Mind Series
ISBN 978-1-947624-00-9 paperback
ISBN 978-1-947624-01-6 ebook

Publisher
Marjorie Lou Ministries
PO Box 75
Seville, FL   32190
www.marjorielou.com

© 2017 by Marjorie Lou Ministries

Printed in the United States of America. All rights reserved under
International Copyright law. Contents and/or cover copy may not be
reproduced in whole or in part in any form without the express written
consent of the Publisher.

Table of Contents

Section One

Introduction 7

Bible Believer 11

What is Renewing the Mind? 19

The Importance of Miracles and Healings 27

You Play a Part 35

How to Use This Book 51

Additional Weapons 57

Section Two

Healings in the Book of Matthew 71

Healings in the Book of Mark 79

Healings in the Book of Luke 85

Healings in the Book of John 91

Miracles in the Book of Matthew 93

Miracles in the Book of Mark 99

Miracles in the Book of Luke 109

Miracles in the Book of John 115

Section One

Dialogue Concerning

Miracles and Healings

Introduction

I love the Word of God so much! It is my life, my breath, my substance; it is everything to me. I eat it, live it, breathe it and love being fully immersed in it. But it was not always so. For many years, I wandered through the lifestyle called "church." I cleaned up my act, gussied myself up and washed out my filthy mouth so I could be accepted into this new intriguing environment I had been introduced into. I gave myself to the Lord, yet there were many areas of my life still all mine. Over the years, God, through His rich mercy, held on to me through tough spots where I could have easily fallen away from the faith. I had no sustenance of my own, no real root in the Word of God. I relied on others to spoon feed me.

As I matured, I began to realize that several people I knew who were very mature in the Lord and very passionate about their walk had conflicting doctrines in particular areas. Each believed the foundational crux of the gospel, of Christ crucified making restitution for our sins. But there were other areas where their interpretation of the Bible differed (which is quite often the case among denominations). This left me in a quandary, because I wanted to know truth. I earnestly desired to walk in truth. But who was correct?

It was time for me to step out from depending on man[1] and begin depending on God Himself. I took all the wonderful teachings of the Word that I had received from men and women throughout the years, and put them on a shelf (so to speak). I did not throw them out since they were still very valuable, but I needed to hear directly from God and know what His truth really is.

Scripture states that the Holy Spirit interprets spiritual things to those who are mature[2] so I put the ball in God's court. Because He is the author and finisher of my faith,[3] He should raise me up to the point of maturity. My part was to be fully yielded and totally obedient to Him.

I have now spent nearly two decades absorbing all He has chosen to teach me, and I know that we have only just begun! The excitement of abiding in this Word, soaking up delicious teachings[4] and revelations has become the greatest adventure! Life in the Kingdom truly amazes me!

It is my heart's desire to impart to you a small portion of the marvelous truth of God's Word that has been revealed, not just to me, but to so many who are seeking understanding at deeper levels. It is time to pull back the veil and glimpse

---

[1] 1 Corinthians 3:2

[2] 1 Corinthians 2:12-13

[3] Hebrews 12:2

[4] Psalms 34:8

some of God's tremendous Glory. I trust you will find it all just as refreshing, exhilarating, and strengthening as I have.

One very important encouragement to you – do not accept anything I say according to my word, but go yourself to *the Word* and to prayer and receive it from God. Searching out the scriptures will open the Word to you and the Holy Spirit Himself will lead you to all truth.[5]

This book is designed to assist Christians with such a process. In it you will find scripture portions to encourage your faith and renew your mind[6] to believe in miracles and experience miracles yourself, enabling you to function as Christ commanded us in the supernatural Kingdom we call "home."

"Lead me in your truth and teach me, for you are the God of my salvation; for you I wait all the day long."

Psalms 25:5

---

[5] John 16:13

[6] Romans 12:2

FOOTNOTES

1 Corinthians 3:2 I fed you with milk, not solid food, for you were not ready for it. And even now you are not yet ready.

[2] 1 Corinthians 2:12-13 Now we have received not the spirit of the world, but the Spirit who is from God, that we might understand the things freely given us by God. And we impart this in words not taught by human wisdom but taught by the Spirit, interpreting spiritual truths to those who are spiritual.

[3] Hebrews 12:2 Looking to Jesus, the founder and perfecter of our faith, who for the joy that was set before him endured the cross, despising the shame, and is seated at the right hand of the throne of God.

[4] Psalms 34:8 Oh, taste and see that the LORD is good! Blessed is the man who takes refuge in him!

[5] John 16:13 When the Spirit of truth comes, he will guide you into all the truth.

[6] Romans 12:2 Do not be conformed to this world, but be transformed by the renewal of your mind, that by testing you may discern what is the will of God, what is good and acceptable and perfect.

Chapter 1

Bible Believer

I appeal to you therefore, brothers, by the mercies of God, to present your bodies as a living sacrifice, holy and acceptable to God, which is your spiritual worship. Do not be conformed to this world but be transformed by the renewal of your mind, that by testing you may discern what is the will of God, what is good and acceptable and perfect.

Romans 12:1-2

Truth be told, I wrote this book for myself. After being challenged with Matthew 17:20 which refers to having only a tiny amount of faith in order to be able to move a mountain, I had to ask myself, "What do I really believe?

I was further challenged with this question one day while standing in my friends' pasture, home to a sweet, long-eared brown donkey. While petting and enjoying this animal, I was surprised by the Lord's sudden challenge to me, "Do you believe this donkey could open his mouth right now and talk like a human? Do you believe I could do that?" I knew this was a reference to Numbers 22:28 where God opened the mouth of Balaam's donkey and it spoke.

I stared at this creature for quite a while, grappling with the question. I did believe God could do it, but right now – out of this donkey's mouth? If I did not believe this, then I could not really believe it about Balaam's donkey either. It was then I began to realize that when reading my Bible, I had no problem believing the donkey spoke, but when standing beside one, I found I did not so readily believe it.

Thus, began a series of testing my internal "believer," where I discovered there were many stories in the Bible I could attest that I believed at a surface level, but when confronted with the physical nature of it, sometimes I had to admit that it was too hard to really believe at a deeper level.

For instance, while frolicking with my family in the ocean one summer, God reminded me that not only did Jesus walk on the stormy sea, but Peter joined him.[7] Walking in the water's edge caused me to be directly confronted with whether I believed that both these men stood on the water and did not sink. Of course, we know that Peter did sink, but only when his mind was distracted by the wind, which caused his focus to be off Jesus for a moment and on his natural circumstances. As soon as he began to sink, his focus was again acutely on Jesus, and Jesus put him right back on top of that water.

---

[7] Matthew 14:22-31

As I stepped in that ocean surf, I had to admit that, though I believe what the Bible says, it was hard to believe these men could step on that water and stay on top of it.

As God exposed numerous areas of unbelief that had been hiding in the dark shadows of my life, I had to consider that maybe this was the reason the truth of the Word was not always being played out in the story of my life. For instance, if Jesus took stripes for my healing, then why was I experiencing a painful frozen shoulder? Why was I laying hands on the sick, but not seeing each one recover?

Although already experiencing small healings, I now realized I had not the faith to cast my mountains into the sea.[8] Just like the man with the epileptic son in Mark 9:24, I found myself crying out, "Lord, I believe! Help me with my unbelief!"

*So faith comes from hearing,
and hearing through the Word of Christ.*

Romans 10:17

---

[8] Matthew 21:21, Mark 11:23

I needed to hear the Word until I really believed it, not just with my head, but at the deeper levels in my spirit. So began my journey of spending time in scriptures that pertain to truths that I struggled to believe. Beginning with the topic of miracles and healing, I focused my Bible reading, meditation and memorization on scriptures that would build my faith to believe for a greater move of the power of God in my life.

In the process, I found it cumbersome to jump around in my Bible to read a portion here, another story there, without it causing distraction to my work. I looked for books already published that would make the process easier, but for all the topical books I found, none had accomplished what I desired. I wanted every verse in the four gospels that pertained to miracles and healing set apart for study.

So, I set out to do the task for myself. I carefully read through the four gospels and isolated every single verse that pertained to my topic. This allowed me to easily spend large amounts of time in these scripture portions, which renewed my mind and planted the truth of God's Word deep within me. As a result, He is now able to manifest greater workings of His power in people's lives by using my yielded life to accomplish His work. In order for me, at His bidding, to lay hands on the sick and they recover, I need to actually believe that with His power I can lay hands on the sick and they will recover. When I do, I am doing the works Jesus did, continuing the work of His Kingdom on earth.

I still use these scriptures today, to constantly refresh my spirit in the truth of God's power. This method has proven so effective that I now want to share with you the scriptures I used to grow my faith for miracles and healings.

And we impart this in words not taught by human wisdom but taught by the Spirit, interpreting spiritual truths to those who are spiritual.

1 Corinthians 2:13

Footnotes

[7] Matthew 14:22-31 Immediately he made the disciples get into the boat and go before him to the other side, while he dismissed the crowds. And after he had dismissed the crowds, he went up on the mountain by himself to pray. When evening came, he was there alone, but the boat by this time was a long way from the land, beaten by the waves, for the wind was against them. And in the fourth watch of the night he came to them, walking on the sea. But when the disciples saw him walking on the sea, they were terrified, and said, "It is a ghost!" and they cried out in fear. But immediately Jesus spoke to them, saying, "Take heart; it is I. Do not be afraid." And Peter answered him, "Lord, if it is you, command me to come to you on the water." He said, "Come." So Peter got out of the boat and walked on the water and came to Jesus. But when he saw the wind, he was afraid, and beginning to sink he cried out, "Lord, save me." Jesus immediately reached out his hand and took hold of him, saying to him, "O you of little faith, why did you doubt?"

[8] Matthew 21:21 And Jesus answered them, "Truly, I say to you, if you have faith and do not doubt, you will not only do what has been done to the fig tree, but even if you say to this mountain, 'Be taken up and thrown into the sea,' it will happen.

[8] Mark 11:23 Truly, I say to you, whoever says to this mountain, 'Be taken up and thrown into the sea,' and does not doubt in his heart, but believes that what he says will come to pass, it will be done for him.

Chapter 2

What is Renewing the Mind?

Do not be conformed to this world, but be transformed by the renewal of your mind, that by testing you may discern what is the will of God, what is good and acceptable and perfect.

Romans 12:2

When we submit ourselves to Jesus Christ, making Him Lord over our lives, He in return makes us a new creation in Him.[9] Our old human nature dies,[10] and we are given the nature of Christ, enabling us to live differently than the rest of the world.

Once we become a new creation in Christ, does that mean that we are all brand new and old habits disappear automatically? That would be great if, when we put off the old man, poof – old habits are gone and new mannerisms and mindsets are automatically "installed on our hard drive!" If we have been born again, made into a new creation, why is it not so easy as this?

---

[9] 2 Corinthians 5:17

[10] Romans 6:4,6

Certainly, we have been translated from the old kingdom of darkness and now walk in His marvelous kingdom.[11] But during our captivity by the enemy we were subjected to a system of brainwashing where we were taught lies and believed them as truth.

Listen to how Paul combats this issue in Ephesians 4:

(20) But that is not the way you learned Christ! –

(21) assuming that you have heard about him and were taught in him, as the truth is in Jesus

(22) to put off your old self, which belongs to your former manner of life and is corrupt through deceitful desires,

(23) and to be renewed in the spirit of your minds,

(24) and to put on the new self, created after the likeness of God in true righteousness and holiness.

Ephesians 4:20-24

Paul gives three steps in a process. The first step (verse 22) is to put off the old man, and the last step (verse 24) is to put on the new man. Sandwiched between these two steps is an interesting requirement for the process - to be renewed in the spirit of your minds.

---

[11] Colossians 1:13

We see essentially the same pattern in the third chapter of Paul's letter to the Colossians:

(9) ... seeing that you have put off the old self with its practices

(10) and have put on the new self, which is being renewed in knowledge after the image of its creator.

Colossians 3:9-10

Just before this passage in Colossians, Paul lists the practices of the old self referring to some of them as "what is earthly in you" (verses 5-8) including such things as anger, malice and slander. Then he makes this statement quoted above (verses 9-10) before going on to tell us the practices we must now put on, such as kindness, humility and patience (verses 12-17). Why did Paul feel the need to insert this passage between our old practices and our new ones?

Paul is teaching us that even though we have been made a new creation, the mind is still used to all the old ways in which we once walked. In order to walk in the new behaviors of the new self we must have our minds renewed in knowledge - meaning the Word of God - so that the transformation process can be completed, making us in the likeness of Jesus Christ.

In order to walk in the new practices that Paul teaches us to "put on," we must be in the Word, being renewed by the Word. Romans 12:2 shows us the transformation is performed by the renewal of our mind. Through the Word we are renewed into the image of Christ[12] and have the mind of Christ.[13]

Brainwashed by the Enemy

*Do not be conformed to this world,
but be transformed by the renewal of your mind...*

Romans 12:2

It commonly occurs with victims rescued out of captivity that they must be "deprogrammed" and therefore require a period of time before they return to normal society. I learned of this phenomena through a friend of mine, Mary Johnston, who was working with a ministry rescuing women out of sex slave trafficking. These women required one to two years and sometimes more just to get their minds renewed in the truth of their value as a person and the correct way to function in normalized societal situations before they would be ready to live freely.

---

[12] Romans 8:29

[13] 1 Corinthians 2:16

Since we have been rescued out of the hands of an enemy, Paul knew we must be renewed in truth to implement the deprogramming required to reverse the damage of the brainwashing we were subjected to by the enemy during our internment. Without this critical step of being renewed in truth, we will not be able to function as a "new man," successfully utilizing our new nature. We instead continue in the old way of thinking and acting.

As with the rescued women, it takes an appropriate period of time for the process of deprogramming to take effect. A quick reading of scriptures "once and you are done" approach will not suffice. You need to stay in the Word until your mind is completely saturated in God's truth so that earthly ways such as anger, slander and obscene talk[14] are no longer resident there. They will be replaced with characteristics of the new nature such as compassion, patience, and kindness.[15]

Once you begin the process, it will take time before you begin to see indications that your mind is being renewed. If you persevere, you will see it. Stick with it and you will slowly be transformed into the likeness of your Savior.

---

[14] Colossians 3:8

[15] Colossians 3:12

I implore you to spend time in the Word. Tarry there so that the truth in it can saturate your mind thereby renewing your mind. Let the life in it transform you into the likeness of the Son of God. Then you will be able to test and know what is the will of God.[16] You will also be able to discern what is good, acceptable and perfect to God, so that you may walk in it. Through the power of the Word, you will break the strongholds the world seems to still have on you and finally put off the old self with its practices. And you will experience the exhilarating freedom of walking in the new self after the image of our Creator. Your human mind will no longer present a barrier to the flow of God's power, making you a prepared vessel ready to experience miracles and healings.

---

[16] Romans 12:2

FOOTNOTES

[9] 2 Corinthians 5:17 Therefore, if anyone is in Christ, he is a new creation. The old has passed away; behold, the new has come.

[10] Romans 6:4,6 We were buried therefore with him by baptism into death, in order that, just as Christ was raised from the dead by the glory of the Father, we too might walk in newness of life…We know that our old self was crucified with him in order that the body of sin might be brought to nothing, so that we would no longer be enslaved to sin.

[11] Colossians 1:13 He has delivered us from the domain of darkness and transferred us to the kingdom of his beloved Son,

[12] Romans 8:29 For those whom he foreknew he also predestined to be conformed to the image of his Son, in order that he might be the firstborn among many brothers.

[13] 1 Corinthians 2:16 "For who has understood the mind of the Lord so as to instruct him?" But we have the mind of Christ.

[14] Colossians 3:8 But now you must put them all away: anger, wrath, malice, slander, and obscene talk from your mouth.

[15] Colossians 3:12 Put on then, as God's chosen ones, holy and beloved, compassionate hearts, kindness, humility, meekness, and patience,

[16] Romans 12:2 Do not be conformed to this world, but be transformed by the renewal of your mind, that by testing you may discern what is the will of God, what is good and acceptable and perfect.

Chapter 3

The Importance of Miracles and Healings

The reason the Son of God appeared was to destroy the works of the devil.

1 John 3:8

With the coming of the Serpent coaxing and deceiving Eve in the Garden of Eden came the beginning of sin and death. God never intended for human beings to cope with sin or death. Included in the process of death is every sickness and disease known to mankind. These things were not created by God, but were a result of the death that Satan brought upon us on that catastrophic day. Even though the bacteria and viruses may have been present for God's good purposes, their ability to affect the human body was not. The human body is designed as a perpetually functioning machine that can continue infinitely. Within our bodies are incredible systems of immunity, intricately designed for our protection. It was only after the fall of man that our bodies became susceptible to processes of dying, as the perpetual system was disrupted and the immunity systems breached, whereby microorganisms could adversely affect us.

Since Jesus came to destroy Satan's works as the scripture passage above tells us, then he came to destroy the work of sickness and disease.

Sickness and disease are not the only "works of the devil" that the earth and its inhabitants have been subjected to, but it is the reason God uses His power for healings. Numerous other problems exist because of the fall of mankind in the garden, including the self-focused nature of people and nature's bondage to corruption that has all creation moaning until it's redemption is complete.[17] In all these areas we see God's hand move in miracles.

Importance of Miracles and Healings in the World

In the Old Testament, every time a great miracle was experienced, the result was the same.

When Elijah called down fire on the alter:

> *And when all the people saw it, they fell on their faces and said, "The LORD, he is God; the LORD, he is God."*
>
> *1 Kings 18:39*

---

[17] Romans 8:20-22

When Daniel interpreted the first dream:

Then King Nebuchadnezzar fell upon his face.... The King answered and said to Daniel, "Truly your God is the God of gods and the Lord of kings..."

Daniel 2:46-47

When Shadrach, Meshach and Abednego survived the fiery furnace, King Nebuchadnezzar declared their God was the "Most High God" and made a decree that no one in the Kingdom could speak against this God. *Daniel 3:26, 29*

When Daniel survived the lions' den, King Darius wrote:

I make a decree, that in all my royal dominion people are to tremble and fear before the God of Daniel, for he is the living God, enduring forever; his kingdom shall never be destroyed, and his dominion shall be to the end. He delivers and rescues; he works signs and wonders in heaven and on earth, he who has saved Daniel from the power of the lions.

Daniel 6:26-27

When the truth of God's Word is manifested before people, they have opportunity to see the reality of the One True God, and fall on their faces and worship Him. Many people have been saved just because they saw miracles or healings. Experiencing or witnessing God's power pushes them past their unbelief. The enemy's works are further destroyed because he is trying desperately to keep people away from God. The signs of miracles or healings draws people closer to God.

> *...God's kindness is meant to lead you to repentance*
>
> Romans 2:4

Importance of Miracles and Healings in Your Household

Once you renew your mind in the truth of miracles and healings, begin to walk in the new nature that Jesus provided to you, and put into practice the power provided to you, your home will never be the same again.

We have seen an abundance of miracles and healings in our family. Our children have little experience with fevers, sore throats, or flu bugs. They cannot relate to the experience referred to as "throwing up" nor have they ever spent prolonged periods of time in bed. They have only had rare trips to the pediatrician that were not "well visits." Even when my son's height was consistently running at 5-10% of average, I laid hands on him every day for 6 months, and less than a year later, he had shot up above the 55% range. The pediatrician had no explanation for me, but I had one for her!

Our children may not be familiar with sickness; however, they can lay hands on the sick and the sick recover. These children have an obvious advantage – they have been raised in a home that believes every word in the Bible and where the truth of the Word has been taught and practiced daily. I understand what Jesus meant when He said you must have the faith of a child to receive the Kingdom of God. Our children believe even when my husband and I struggle to believe. They are perplexed only when the healing *doesn't* happen.

When my son was eight years old, he was stabbed in the eye with a fork and was bleeding from the eyeball. Within 10 minutes, the eye was healed and snow white with absolutely no watery red irritation. All that remained of the incident was a red speck on the eyeball where the fork penetrated and the bloody stains down the front of his shirt. When we saw the miracle God had done, we spent the next two hours praising and worshiping God in our living room floor. Since then, we have shared this story with all who will listen and God's glory has been revealed to many skeptical individuals, breaking down strongholds the enemy had on them preventing them from believing in the power of our mighty God.

As we share this and other stories from within our home, we find that others respond just like in the Old Testament stories. Neighbors, friends and extended family may refute the idea of Jesus Christ, but they cannot deny our testimony. When people hear our stories they are amazed, strongholds are broken, and people are healed. Later, when they need a miracle and do not have the faith to believe God's Word for their situation, they seek us out. This opens the door for the fullness of the gospel to be presented and penetrate their hearts. In this way, God's work in our household spills out into the community revealing Jesus Christ to many who previously had rejected Him.[18]

God provides full protection for your household through the finished work of the cross. It is available, but you must learn how to partake of it. The Devil tells you that you cannot have this for your family, but he is only attempting to keep you away from God's truth. Do not believe him when he whispers to you that it is too late. Anyone who believes God's Word and walks under God's authority has this immeasurable greatness of power made available to them.[19]

It is up to you to begin the process of renewing your mind after the image of your creator[20] by spending time in the scriptures provided in this book. Put your hand to the plow and do not look back.[21] Once the truth of His Word penetrates deep into your spirit, you too will begin to see God's hand moving, and the resulting testimonies will affect your world for Jesus Christ.

---

[18] For more testimonies please visit KingdomPurposeLife.com/testimony

Share your testimony by emailing testimony@KingdomPurposeLife.com

[19] Ephesians 1:19

[20] Colossians 3:10

[21] Luke 9:62

*And they went out and preached everywhere,
while the Lord worked with them
and confirmed the message by accompanying signs.*

Mark 16:20

FOOTNOTES

[17] Romans 8:20-22 For the creation was subjected to futility, not willingly, but because of him who subjected it, in hope that the creation itself will be set free from its bondage to corruption and obtain the freedom of the glory of the children of God. For we know that the whole creation has been groaning together in the pains of childbirth until now.

[19] Ephesians 1:19 and what is the immeasurable greatness of his power toward us who believe, according to the working of his great might

[20] Colossians 3:10 and have put on the new self, which is being renewed in knowledge after the image of its creator.

[21] Luke 9:62 Jesus said to him, "No one who puts his hand to the plow and looks back is fit for the kingdom of God."

Chapter 4

You Play a Part

*Therefore I tell you, whatever you ask in prayer,
Believe that you have received it,
And it will be yours.*

Mark 11:24

There is a part you and I must play to effectuate God's truth into our lives. But to accomplish our part requires that we believe every word spoken by God. How often do we not believe what we read in the Bible because we are not seeing it in our circumstances? For instance, we say that we believe Jesus bore stripes for our healing[22] but when our circumstances bear us a sore throat, we find that we do not so readily believe His stripes provided our healing. After all, that throat really does hurt!

Jesus Himself taught us the secret to receiving all that the Word has provided to us. We must first believe we have already received it, *then* we will see it.

Wait a minute! Isn't that putting the cart before the

---

[22] 1 Peter 2:24

horse? I mean, if I have a sore throat, Jesus is telling me that I must believe it is already healed, *then* it will be healed. But it is not healed until I see that it is no longer inflamed!

When you process Jesus' statement in our natural way of thinking, it does not make much sense. It is a humanly impossible task, but Jesus would not tell us to do something that was impossible.

> *With man this is impossible,*
> *but with God all things are possible*
>
> Matthew 19:26

When you try to believe in human terms, you will experience human failure. God's truth must be effectuated by God's methods. He alone knows how His truths can become real in a human being. When you allow Him to lead you into His truth, He is then able to set you free from the captivity of sin and death.[23]

Therefore, renewing the mind is vitally important. In Jesus' mind, sickness is a work of the enemy that He came to destroy. Once we begin renewing our mind, we will begin to think like Jesus thinks, because we will have the mind of Christ.[24] We will see sickness, not as something that we are

---

[23] Including sickness

[24] 1 Corinthians 2:16

victim to, but as something that has no more power to victimize us. Once you believe that Jesus took stripes for your healing, you will feel the sore throat and respond, "That's not possible! Jesus already came to destroy that work!" Then in your belief of His Word, you will rebuke that sore throat, just like Jesus rebuked the fever in Luke 4:39. Just like that fever, the sore throat will flee.

Who, Me?

Miracles and healings are for anyone who will trust God at his word. Many people reason that miracles and healings are only for special people God isolates for that job. It is true, God does use certain people to operate in miracles so that people may see and believe, but He does not limit His power to these people only.

And these signs will accompany those who believe:
in my name they will cast out demons;
they will speak in new tongues;
...they will lay their hands on the sick, and they will recover.

Mark 16:17-18

The scripture above is taken from the great commission as recorded in the book of Mark. These are Jesus' final words as He departed this Earth.

We learn in verse 14 that Jesus speaks these words directly to His eleven disciples. (At this point, there are no longer twelve disciples as Judas, one of the twelve, is now dead.)[25] Jesus begins by rebuking them for unbelief and hardness of heart because they did not at first believe the reports of Jesus rising from the dead. Jesus is preparing them, as there would be no way they would be able to obey the words Jesus was about to speak to them if they still had unbelief. Immediately after this rebuke, He begins the passage of scripture that we commonly refer to as the "great commission."

Although He addresses the eleven disciples directly, verse 17 clearly reveals who Jesus is sending out to fulfill this commission – *those who believe.*

I believe upon the great, mighty name of Jesus Christ for my salvation, for from no other will I find righteousness. Most assuredly I will not find righteousness in my own efforts. Not even from the greatest work that I do for His Kingdom will I find salvation, for the word proclaims that all my righteous deeds are completely useless trash.[26] The word does not say my horrible deeds are trash, it says all my *righteous* deeds are completely useless to Him. I must believe on Him, trusting that He has imparted to me His righteousness, and do all my works in and through Him. Since I believe this, I am included in the group Jesus refers to as "those who believe."

---

[25] Matthew 27:3-5

[26] Isaiah 64:6

Because I believe, Jesus commissions me to take the gospel to all the world, and to expect certain supernatural signs to follow me as I go. If you read on to verse 20, you find the importance of these signs.

*And they went out and preached everywhere,
while the Lord worked with them
and confirmed the message by accompanying signs.*

Mark 16:20

The supernatural signs confirm the word that is being spoken, and open people's eyes to glimpse the reality of God's Kingdom. Your part is to take the gospel and speak it. Jesus' part is to confirm your words as being really His words by giving accompanying signs.

We find other scripture references where Jesus commands His followers to take such actions in His name.

*And he called to him his twelve disciples
and gave them authority over unclean spirits,
to cast them out,
and to heal every disease and every affliction.*

*And proclaim as you go, saying,
'The kingdom of heaven is at hand.'
Heal the sick,
raise the dead,
cleanse lepers,
cast out demons.*

Matthew 10:1, 7-8

Are you surprised at the list of activities Jesus is sending out his disciples to perform? Every act listed in this passage of scripture is nothing short of miraculous - supernatural, beyond our human abilities. In essence, Jesus commands us to go out and do miracles.

This is not a list of actions Jesus sends the super-anointed exceptional pastors or evangelists to do. He tells *you* to do it. Everything on this list your King Jesus Christ commanded and He is expecting you to comply in obedience. Jesus Christ tells you to go out and proclaim the gospel, heal the sick, raise the dead, cleanse diseases and cast out demons. This is what Jesus expects your Christian life to look like. If you walk in obedience to this mandate from heaven, you will be an obedient servant in the house of God.

Has the LORD as great delight in burnt offerings and sacrifices,
as in obeying the voice of the LORD?
Behold, to obey is better than sacrifice,
and to listen than the fat of rams.

1 Samuel 15:22

Do you believe? Are you a believer in Jesus Christ? If your answer is "yes," then Jesus commissions you to go out and do what He commanded you to accomplish. As you go, expect and trust that He will work with you and confirm your message through miraculous signs.

Free Will

What challenging words Jesus left us with as He departed the Earth! Although He was going again back to the Father, He still had work to be accomplished here, so He left a commission for generations of believers to come, directing them in their number one priority in His Kingdom – taking the gospel into all the world so that all may hear.

This is your mandate, and with your mandate firmly established, you must decide how you will spend the appointed days, hours, minutes you have been given on the earth at this very point in history. Do you see your family time, or work time, or free time as pursuits of earthly needs and pleasures? Or are you seeking first the Kingdom of God, trusting all those needs will be added unto you? Are you focused on your King, pursuing the Kingdom work He has laid out for you to accomplish in the place where He has established you?

The essence of free will lies in this critical decision of how you will spend your earthly time. The question is not whether you will choose to go out and sin or not, but rather, whether you will stop judging what constitutes sin and completely surrender yourself to what the King wills for your life. This is what Jesus Himself was deciding when He proclaimed, "Not my will, but yours, Father!"[27]

---

[27] Matthew 26:39

Perhaps this is one of the reasons Jesus said the way into the gate of life is narrow, and few there be that find it.[28]

Benefits of Choosing the Kingdom

Everyone will make two choices during their life. No one escapes these decisions:

> Will you believe on Jesus Christ for your righteousness unto salvation?
>
> If you believe, will you lay down your life and follow Him?

If upon weighing the cost you choose to answer "yes" to each of these questions, then you will take your part in the history of mankind as a participant in a Kingdom that brings glory to God.

> *By this my Father is glorified,*
> *that you bear much fruit*
> *and so prove to be my disciples.*
>
> *John 15:8*

---

[28] Matthew 7:14

Here are just a few of the many benefits of choosing to follow God's will and live your life experiencing miracles and healings.

The Kingdom of God is activated.

In my book, "*Power of the Kingdom*," I explain in detail how God utilizes people to work His power here on Earth.[29] He has made an immeasurable greatness of His power available to those who believe.[30] But He is relying on you to get up and use it for His purposes. When Jesus' people choose to live their lives for a Kingdom purpose, Jesus' work is continuing to be accomplished on this earth.

People Believe

Whenever God confirms His Word with the accompanying signs, people see the gospel in action and they believe. Many come to salvation as a result, and the Kingdom grows. Consequently, there are more believers doing Kingdom work; therefore, more work is being accomplished, the gospel spreads, and God's magnificent glory is manifested.

---

[29] Free copy at KingdomPurposeLife.com/free-ebook-power-kingdom

[30] Ephesians 1:19

Satan Defeated

Do you know how important your testimony is? Every time Jesus works with you by showing accompanying signs, you have another addition to your testimony! Once you grasp the power of it, you will be looking for every opportunity to build it up.

Why is your testimony so valuable?

And they have conquered him
by the blood of the lamb
and by the word of their testimony

Revelation 12:11

Your testimony plays a part in the defeat of Satan. Because of the sacrifice of Jesus Christ, the blood of the lamb which was spilt for you, you are made ready and able to utilize the authority handed to you: authority over unclean spirits, diseases and any other work of the enemy.[31] This stops Satan in his tracks, preventing his schemes from succeeding in your life.

---

[31] Matthew 10:1

Revival

Hundreds of thousands, if not millions, of people throughout many generations have prayed for revival yet never saw results from their prayers. I cannot help but wonder how many of them would have experienced great revival had they prioritized walking out Jesus' great commission in their lives. When you go out and heal the sick or raise the dead, it causes an eruption of attention on the gospel and the Holy Spirit can prick the conscience. Many a revival was stirred, not by cleaver marketing strategies to manipulate a "movement," but by simple ordinary people with a testimony taking the gospel to the people. Once the accompanying signs begin to manifest, the word spreads, people are attracted, and they begin falling on their knees when they see the majestic, powerful, Almighty One He is!

Bear Much Fruit

A tremendous benefit of choosing a Kingdom purpose life is the resulting fruit you bear. When sickness arises in our home, every member of our family understands that it is not God's work, but the enemy's, and every one of us knows how to wield the Word of God as a sword and attack that enemy to stop him. Fevers, sore throats, flu bugs, cancer have no authority over our house, because we serve a God who is more powerful than those things, and we believe His word, that His authority has been granted to us to cast them out.[32]

Remember the story about when my son was stabbed in the eyeball with a fork? We prayed with the authority given to us by Jesus Christ, and Jesus healed that eye in less than ten minutes. His vision is perfect, and there are no repercussions of any form. The result? We have shared that testimony anywhere we could, and brought great glory to God before many people, bearing much fruit in the Kingdom of God. And my son was spared from living with a blind eye for the rest of his life.

Those Glorious Words!

There is one thing I live for in my life and everything about my life is designed to meet this one goal – and that is to hear these words:

> *His master said to him,*
> *'Well done, good and faithful servant.*
> *You have been faithful over a little;*
> *I will set you over much.*
> *Enter into the joy of your master.'*
>
> Matthew 25:21

---

[32] Matthew 10:8

Nothing else matters but to hear Jesus say these words to me on the appointed day. My marriage, my parenting, my work, my relationships with others – I live out all these things with a Kingdom mindset doing all that Jesus has commanded me to do, and apply it to all these areas of my life.

This is the reason I spent so much time renewing my mind in the Word of God, so that I am a ready, able and yielded vessel to take the gospel to the world and operate in the accompanying signs that Jesus uses to confirm my word as His Word. Then one day I will hear, "Well done! Enter into the joy of your Master!" That is where I plan to spend eternity – in the joy of my Master.

It's Time to Prepare

You would not expect to enjoy success at a new job unless you are properly trained in the skills needed to accomplish the required tasks. No student sits down to take a major academic test without spending many untold hours studying and preparing, if they have any hope of receiving an acceptable grade. Nor should you expect signs to follow you as you share the Gospel unless you have spent adequate time renewing your mind.

Remember the passage we looked at in the beginning of this chapter? It was the passage commonly referred to as the great commission as recorded in Mark, chapter 16. Before

Jesus gave the great commission, he rebuked the disciples for their unbelief and hardness of heart. These men had been by Jesus' side as He performed miracle after miracle, yet they still struggled to believe. We also have unbelief and hardness of heart, as evidenced by our inability to walk in the miracles Jesus did. Even as I tell my story, I still deal with unbelief and hardness of heart at many levels, and like the disciples, must continue the process of rooting it out.

Only the Word of God can correct this condition in mankind. We have been programmed into unbelief by the world, and only the Word can deprogram us so that we are able to believe. We must take off the old man with its ways of thinking, but that old nature does not let go so readily. Only the Word of God has the power to break that stronghold over us and set us free in the truth of Jesus Christ.

Now it is up to you. Will you hear the voice of your Master and obey the commission you have been assigned in the Kingdom? Will you complete the task at hand, doing service for your King? Or will you continue in the natural life, chasing your tail in pursuit of things that have no eternal value?

If you choose the Kingdom life, then your first step in preparing yourself is to begin renewing your mind in the Word of God, building up your inner man and armoring yourself with the belt of truth.[33] Renewing your mind in the area of miracles and healings is a great place to begin.

---

[33] Ephesians 6:14

FOOTNOTES

[22] 1 Peter 2:24 He himself bore our sins in his body on the tree, that we might die to sin and live to righteousness. By his wounds you have been healed

[24] 1 Corinthians 2:16 "For who has understood the mind of the Lord so as to instruct him?" But we have the mind of Christ.

[25] Matthew 27:3-5 Then when Judas, his betrayer, saw that Jesus was condemned, he changed his mind and brought back the thirty pieces of silver to the chief priests and the elders, saying, "I have sinned by betraying innocent blood." They said, "What is that to us? See to it yourself." And throwing down the pieces of silver into the temple, he departed, and he went and hanged himself.

[26] Isaiah 64:6 We have all become like one who is unclean, and all our righteous deeds are like a polluted garment. We all fade like a leaf, and our iniquities, like the wind, take us away.

[27] Matthew 26:39 And going a little farther he fell on his face and prayed, saying, "My Father, if it be possible, let this cup pass from me; nevertheless, not as I will, but as you will."

[28] Matthew 7:14 For the gate is narrow and the way is hard that leads to life, and those who find it are few.

[30] Ephesians 1:19 and what is the immeasurable greatness of his power toward us who believe, according to the working of his great might.

[31] Matthew 10:1 And he called to him his twelve disciples and gave them authority over unclean spirits, to cast them out, and to heal every disease and every affliction.

[32] Matthew 10:8 Heal the sick, raise the dead, cleanse lepers, cast out demons. You received without paying; give without pay.

[33] Ephesians 6:14 Stand therefore, having fastened on the belt of truth, and having put on the breastplate of righteousness,

Chapter 5

How to Use This Book

This publication is designed to assist you in renewing your mind specifically for believing for miracles and healing. Portions of scriptures pertinent to this subject are compiled for your convenience, implementing personal study and facilitating saturation of these words until your mind grasps the truths within. You will enjoy reading the scriptures without the task of finding and isolating them.

I have included in this book all the verses I felt would contribute to renewing your mind in miracles and healings. Each gospel is divided into two sections – one for miracles and one for healings. Occasionally I have included the same passage in both sections to make it more congruent.

There are several ways to utilize this book.

Reference Guide

This publication serves as a handy reference guide for finding scriptures specific to miracles and healings. It facilitates a quick read of the topic for study or general reference.

Isolated Reading

This book provides opportunity to read quickly through the topical scriptures to become familiar with them, without spending huge amounts of time searching for them. By isolating these scriptures, your mind is not distracted.

Soaking in the Word

Although quickly reading through this book will assist you in seeing the truth, I recommend that you spend lengthy periods of time soaking in this heavenly manna, savoring the delicious fruit so that you may finally taste and see the richness of His goodness while at the same time renewing your mind into the likeness of Christ in this particular topic.

One way to do this is simply reading passages over and over. Perhaps there is a portion that specifically sticks out to you. Read that portion numerous times. To spend days, weeks or months on one particular passage may be just what the Holy Spirit needs you to do so that He can begin to interpret His truths to you.

Another way to absorb the scriptures is through memorization. By hiding the Word in your heart, you have a storehouse inside you stocked full of truth that you can pull up at any time when you need an answer to a problem in your life, or that the Holy Spirit can bring to your remembrance when He wants to reveal more of Jesus to you. In addition, the Holy Spirit has ammunition to utilize when the enemy attacks you. You are then able to wield the Word as a true sword of the Spirit, speaking out God's truth and stopping the enemy in his tracks.

A powerful way to assimilate the Word is to take a passage and read it over and over, each time accentuating a different word in the passage. You will be surprised just how much this will assist your understanding of the passage.

For instance, if you wanted you soak in a portion of scripture from John 14:12, you would start by accentuating the first word of the passage:

> ***Whoever*** *believes in me will also do the works that I do*

Let it soak in. Let the meaning of *whoever* really come to you. Then read the passage again, accentuating the second word this time:

> *Whoever **believes** in me will also do the works that I do*

Once you have grasped the meaning of this word in the passage, move to the next word:

> *Whoever believes **in** me will also do the works that I do*

And again:

> *Whoever believes in **me** will also do the works that I do*

Continue this process until you have completed the whole passage. By the time you complete the process, you will understand this passage at a whole new level. The Lord will begin to show you deeper truths that you had simply read over before. As an added benefit, you will probably have the passage memorized!

Another way to soak in the Word is to take enough time to let a picture form in your mind. Use your imagination to see the scene played out. Ask God to formulate the scene for you in your mind.

Once you have tarried in these passages long enough, the truth of it will penetrate past the blockage of your mind's natural way of thinking. The de-programming will begin as the transformation takes shape. The Spirit of God will interpret spiritual things to you.[34] You will begin to see the process of the "new self" emerging as the "old self" is taken off.[35]

As you utilize this book, I pray that our Lord will open the eyes of your understanding filling you with truth and wisdom so that you may be able to walk as Jesus walked and do the works that He did.[36]

---

[34] 1 Corinthians 2:13

[35] Ephesians 4:20-24

[36] Ephesians 1:18

FOOTNOTES

[34] I Corinthians 2:13 And we impart this in words not taught by human wisdom but taught by the Spirit, interpreting spiritual truths to those who are spiritual.

[35] Ephesians 4:20-24 But that is not the way you learned Christ!— assuming that you have heard about him and were taught in him, as the truth is in Jesus, to put off your old self, which belongs to your former manner of life and is corrupt through deceitful desires, and to be renewed in the spirit of your minds, and to put on the new self, created after the likeness of God in true righteousness and holiness.

[36] Ephesians 1:18 having the eyes of your hearts enlightened, that you may know what is the hope to which he has called you, what are the riches of his glorious inheritance in the saints,

Chapter 6

Additional Weapons

And take...the sword of the Spirit, which is the Word of God.

Ephesians 6:17

In addition to the scriptures in the four Gospels pertaining to miracles and healings, there are other scriptures that are worthy for renewing your mind. In addition, these scriptures serve as loaded weapons, ready to fire at the enemy at the first sign of fiery darts.[37]

Jesus Christ did much more than just rescue us out the hands of the enemy, He placed in our hands weaponry effective against further attacks from this enemy. He placed in our hand a sword more powerful than any military arsenal. Having paid a huge price to provide us this supernatural sword, He fully expects us to wield it skillfully.

New military enlistees must first go to boot camp, or a training camp, before they are ready to work in any field of the Armed Forces. A crucial part of the training they receive is with their weapons. Although they do train in firing and target accuracy, the most extensive training is in weapon

---

[37] Ephesians 6:16

mastery. They must know their weapon inside-out in order that, on the battlefield, they will have their full mental capacity trained on the circumstance and not have to be thinking about their weapon during a high-intensity situation.

As with the soldier training to use his weapon for battle, learning to use the Word as a weapon requires great time and practice to become so familiar with it that you use it without thinking about the weapon, only about the situation you are dealing with.

Whenever the enemy attempts to get you to believe anything that is contrary to the Word of God, you strike him with the sword of the Spirit. Any time you are having thoughts that do not agree with the Word of God, speak these words of truth. Once the reality of these truths become real inside you, believing mixes with the spoken word. It is then that the strike from that sword becomes a deadly blow.

Most of the following passages of scripture have become regular everyday vernacular for me, being woven in my conversations and spoken out loud as I walk, work, play or drive.

The following scriptures are by no means exclusive, but are some of my favorite and most used weapons against the enemy. With them, you will begin the process of building your own arsenal against Satan.

Weapons

My first and favorite weapon is Psalm 91. I have spent more time in this Psalm than any other, because it is rich with blessing and protection against the enemy, and because it took time to soak in it enough to deprogram my mind and be able to believe every word. I do not recall a time when I used the entire Psalm at once, but I find that for most situations I face, it is rare that I do not pull some portion of this powerful arsenal to speak out and stop the enemy.

> He who dwells in the shelter of the Most High
> > will abide in the shadow of the Almighty.
>
> I will say to the LORD, "My refuge and my fortress,
> > my God, in whom I trust."
>
> For he will deliver you from the snare of the fowler
> > and from the deadly pestilence.
>
> He will cover you with his pinions,
> > and under his wings you will find refuge;
> > his faithfulness is a shield and buckler.
>
> You will not fear the terror of the night,
> > nor the arrow that flies by day,
>
> nor the pestilence that stalks in darkness,
> > nor the destruction that wastes at noonday.
>
> A thousand may fall at your side,
> > ten thousand at your right hand,
> > but it will not come near you.
>
> You will only look with your eyes
> > and see the recompense of the wicked.

Because you have made the LORD your dwelling place—
>   the Most High, who is my refuge—
no evil shall be allowed to befall you,
>   no plague come near your tent.
For he will command his angels concerning you
>   to guard you in all your ways.
On their hands they will bear you up,
>   lest you strike your foot against a stone.
You will tread on the lion and the adder;
>   the young lion and the serpent you will trample underfoot.
"Because he holds fast to me in love, I will deliver him;
I will protect him, because he knows my name.
 When he calls to me, I will answer him;
>   I will be with him in trouble;
>   I will rescue him and honor him.
With long life I will satisfy him
>   and show him my salvation.

Psalm 91

Another powerful scripture for your arsenal is Psalm 23. I find the Holy Spirit leading me to use portions of this passage frequently, both in praise and in warfare.

> The LORD is my shepherd; I shall not want.
>> He makes me lie down in green pastures.
> He leads me beside still waters.
>> He restores my soul.
> He leads me in paths of righteousness
>> for his name's sake.
> Even though I walk through the valley of the shadow of death,
>> I will fear no evil,
> for you are with me;
>> your rod and your staff,
>> they comfort me.
> You prepare a table before me
>> in the presence of my enemies;
> you anoint my head with oil;
>> my cup overflows.
> Surely goodness and mercy shall follow me
>> all the days of my life,
> and I shall dwell in the house of the LORD
>> forever.

Psalm 23

Another critical passage is the list of the blessings for obedience. Since our obedience is now in Jesus Christ and he already took the curse for us by being hung on a cross,[38] all that is left for us is the blessings. When Satan tries to trick you into believing the list of curses are happening to you, it is powerful to know these blessings. (You can read the list of curses starting in verse 15 so that you recognize them, but you do not need to spend time there; they are not for you if you are in Christ Jesus.)

> Blessed shall you be in the city, and blessed shall you be in the field.
>
> Blessed shall be the fruit of your womb and the fruit of your ground and the fruit of your cattle, the increase of your herds and the young of your flock.
>
> Blessed shall be your basket and your kneading bowl.
>
> Blessed shall you be when you come in, and blessed shall you be when you go out.
>
> "The LORD will cause your enemies who rise against you to be defeated before you. They shall come out against you one way and flee before you seven ways.

---

[38] Galatians 3:13

The Lord will command the blessing on you in your barns and in all that you undertake. And he will bless you in the land that the Lord your God is giving you.

The Lord will establish you as a people holy to himself, as he has sworn to you, if you keep the commandments of the Lord your God and walk in his ways. And all the peoples of the earth shall see that you are called by the name of the Lord, and they shall be afraid of you.

And the Lord will make you abound in prosperity, in the fruit of your womb and in the fruit of your livestock and in the fruit of your ground, within the land that the Lord swore to your fathers to give you.

The Lord will open to you his good treasury, the heavens, to give the rain to your land in its season and to bless all the work of your hands.

And you shall lend to many nations, but you shall not borrow.

And the Lord will make you the head and not the tail, and you shall only go up and not down.

Deuteronomy 28:3-13

More Powerful Scriptures

The following are a few of my most heavily used weapons:

> No weapon formed against you shall prosper,
> And every tongue which rises against you in judgment you shall condemn.
> This is the heritage of the servants of the LORD,
> And their righteousness is from Me,"
> Says the LORD.
>
> Isaiah 54:17 (NKJV)

Christ redeemed us from the curse of the law by becoming a curse for us—for it is written, "Cursed is everyone who is hanged on a tree"—

Galatians 3:13

Who his own self bare our sins in his own body on the tree, that we, being dead to sins, should live unto righteousness:

by whose stripes you were healed.

1 Peter 2:24 (NKJV)

And we know that for those who love God all things work together for good, for those who are called according to his purpose.

Romans 8:28

I have been crucified with Christ. It is no longer I who live, but Christ who lives in me.

Galatians 2:20

But the fruit of the Spirit is love, joy, peace, patience, kindness, goodness, faithfulness, gentleness, self-control; against such things there is no law.

Galatians 5:22-23

What then shall we say to these things? If God is for us, who can be against us? He who did not spare his own Son but gave him up for us all, how will he not also with him graciously give us all things?

Who shall bring any charge against God's elect? It is God who justifies. Who is to condemn?

Christ Jesus is the one who died—more than that, who was raised—who is at the right hand of God, who indeed is interceding for us.

Who shall separate us from the love of Christ? Shall tribulation, or distress, or persecution, or famine, or nakedness, or danger, or sword? As it is written,

"For your sake we are being killed all the day long;

we are regarded as sheep to be slaughtered."

No, in all these things we are more than conquerors through him who loved us.

For I am sure that neither death nor life, nor angels nor rulers, nor things present nor things to come, nor powers, nor height nor depth, nor anything else in all creation, will be able to separate us from the love of God in Christ Jesus our Lord.

Romans 8:31-39

…having the eyes of your hearts enlightened, that you may know what is the hope to which he has called you, what are the riches of his glorious inheritance in the saints, and what is the immeasurable greatness of his power toward us who believe, according to the working of his great might that he worked in Christ when he raised him from the dead

Ephesians 1:18-20

Now to him who is able to do far more abundantly than all that we ask or think, according to the power at work within us, to him be glory in the church and in Christ Jesus throughout all generations, forever and ever. Amen.

Ephesians 3:20-21

Final Thought

Any time you pull out these weapons for use, Satan will try to convince you they will not work. As you speak out these powerful words of God, you must remember He is waiting for you to speak them out in faith so that He can perform them.

Then the LORD said to me, "You have seen well, for I am watching over my word to perform it."

Jeremiah 1:12

FOOTNOTES

[37] Ephesians 6:16 In all circumstances take up the shield of faith, with which you can extinguish all the flaming darts of the evil one;

[38] Galatians 3:13 Christ redeemed us from the curse of the law by becoming a curse for us—for it is written, "Cursed is everyone who is hanged on a tree"—

Section Two

Scripture References For

Miracles and Healings

Healings

The Gospel According to
Matthew

And he went throughout all Galilee, teaching in their synagogues and proclaiming the gospel and healing every disease and every affliction among the people. So his fame spread throughout all Syria, and they brought him all the sick, those afflicted with various diseases and pains, those oppressed by demons, epileptics and paralytics, and he healed them.

Matthew 4:23-24

When he came down from the mountain, great crowds followed him. And behold, a leper came to him and knelt before him saying, "Lord, if you will, you can make me clean." And Jesus stretched out his hand and touched him saying, "I will; be clean." And immediately his leprosy was cleansed.

Matthew 8:1-3

When he entered Capernaum, a centurion came forward to him, appealing to him, "Lord, my servant is lying paralyzed at home, suffering terribly." And he said, "I will come and heal him. But the Centurion replied, "Lord, I am not worthy to have you come under my roof, but say the word, and my servant will be healed.... And to the centurion Jesus said, "Go; let it be done for you as you have believed." And the servant was healed at that very moment.

> Matthew 8:5-8, 13

That evening they brought to him many who were oppressed by demons, and he cast out the spirits with a word and healed all who were sick. This was to fulfill what was spoken by the prophet Isaiah: "He took our illnesses and bore our diseases."

> Matthew 8:16-17

And behold, some people brought to him a paralytic, lying on a bed. And when Jesus saw their faith, he said to the paralytic, "Take heart, my son; your sins are forgiven." And behold, some of the scribes said to themselves, "This man is blaspheming." But Jesus, knowing their thoughts, said, "Why do you think evil in your hearts? For which is easier, to say, 'Your sins are forgiven,' or to say, 'Rise and walk?' But that you may know that the Son of Man has authority on earth to forgive sins" —he then said to the paralytic— "Rise, pick up your bed and go home." And he rose and went home.

> Matthew 9:2-7

And behold, a woman who had suffered from a discharge of blood for twelve years came up behind him and touched the fringe of his garment, for she said to herself, "If I only touch his garment, I will be made well." Jesus turned, and seeing her he said, "Take heart, daughter; your faith has made you well. "And instantly the woman was made well.

                                            Matthew 9:20-22

And as Jesus passed on from there, two blind men followed him, crying aloud, "Have mercy on us, Son of David." When he entered the house, the blind men came to him, and Jesus said to them, "Do you believe that I am able to do this?" They said to him, "Yes, Lord." Then he touched their eyes, saying, "According to your faith be it done to you." And their eyes were opened.

                                            Matthew 9:27-30

As they were going away, behold, a demon-oppressed man who was mute was brought to him. And when the demon had been cast out, the mute man spoke.

                                            Matthew 9:32-33

And Jesus went throughout all the cities and villages, teaching in their synagogues and proclaiming the gospel of the kingdom and healing every disease and every affliction.

                                            Matthew 9:35

And he called to him his twelve disciples and gave them authority over unclean spirits, to cast them out, and to heal every disease and every affliction…And proclaim as you go, saying, 'The kingdom of heaven is at hand.' Heal the sick, raise the dead, cleanse lepers, cast out demons.

Matthew 10:1, 7-8

And Jesus answered them, "Go and tell John what you hear and see: the blind receive their sight and the lame walk, lepers are cleansed and the deaf hear, and the dead are raised up,

Matthew 11:4-5

And a man was there with a withered hand… Then he said to the man, "Stretch out your hand." And the man stretched it out, and it was restored, healthy like the other.

Matthew 12:10, 13

Many followed him, and he healed them all.

Matthew 12:15

Then a demon-oppressed man who was blind and mute was brought to him, and he healed him, so that the man spoke and saw.

Matthew 12:22

When he went ashore he saw a great crowd, and he had compassion on them and healed their sick.

Matthew 14:14

And when the men of that place recognized him, they sent around to all that region and brought to him all who were sick and implored him that they might only touch the fringe of his garment. And as many as touched it were made well.

Matthew 14:35-36

And behold, a Canaanite woman from that region came out and was crying, "Have mercy on me, O Lord, Son of David; my daughter is severely oppressed by a demon." But he did not answer her a word. And his disciples came and begged him, saying, "Send her away, for she is crying out after us." He answered, "I was sent only to the lost sheep of the house of Israel." But she came and knelt before him, saying, "Lord, help me." And he answered, "It is not right to take the children's bread and throw it to the dogs." She said, "Yes, Lord, yet even the dogs eat the crumbs that fall from their masters' table." Then Jesus answered her, "O woman, great is your faith! Be it done for you as you desire." And her daughter was healed instantly.

Matthew 15:22-28

And great crowds came to him, bringing with them the lame, the blind, the crippled, the mute, and many others, and they put them at his feet, and he healed them, so that the crowd wondered, when they saw the mute speaking, the crippled healthy, the lame walking, and the blind seeing. And they glorified the God of Israel.

        Matthew 15:30-31

And when they came to the crowd, a man came up to him and, kneeling before him, said, "Lord, have mercy on my son, for he is an epileptic and he suffers terribly. For often he falls into the fire, and often into the water. And I brought him to your disciples, and they could not heal him." And Jesus answered, "O faithless and twisted generation, how long am I to be with you? How long am I to bear with you? Bring him here to me." And Jesus rebuked the demon, and it came out of him, and the boy was healed instantly.

        Matthew 17:14-18

And large crowds followed him, and he healed them there.

        Matthew 19:2

And behold, there were two blind men sitting by the roadside, and when they heard that Jesus was passing by, they cried out, "Lord, have mercy on us, Son of David!" The crowd rebuked them, telling them to be silent, but they cried out all the more, "Lord, have mercy on us, Son of David!" And stopping, Jesus called them and said, "What do you want me to do for you?" They said to him, "Lord, let our eyes be opened." And Jesus in pity touched their eyes, and immediately they recovered their sight and followed him.

Matthew 20:30-34

And the blind and the lame came to him in the temple, and he healed them.

Matthew 21:14

Healings

The Gospel According to
Mark

Now Simon's mother-in-law lay ill with a fever, and immediately they told him about her. And he came and took her by the hand and lifted her up, and the fever left her, and she began to serve them.

Mark 1:30-31

That evening at sundown they brought to him all who were sick or oppressed by demons. And the whole city was gathered together at the door. And he healed many who were sick with various diseases, and cast out many demons.

Mark 1:32-34

And a leper came to him, imploring him, and kneeling said to him, "If you will, you can make me clean." Moved with pity, he stretched out his hand and touched him and said to him, "I will; be clean." And immediately the leprosy left him, and he was made clean.

Mark 1:40-42

And they came, bringing to him a paralytic carried by four men. And when they could not get near him because of the crowd, they removed the roof above him, and when they had made an opening, they let down the bed on which the paralytic lay. And when Jesus saw their faith, he said to the paralytic, "Son, your sins are forgiven."… "But that you may know that the Son of Man has authority on earth to forgive sins" —he said to the paralytic— "I say to you, rise, pick up your bed, and go home." And he rose and immediately picked up his bed and went out before them all.

> Mark 2:3-5, 10-12

Again he entered the synagogue, and a man was there with a withered hand. And they watched Jesus, to see whether he would heal him on the Sabbath, so that they might accuse him. And he said to the man with the withered hand, "Come here." And he said to them, "Is it lawful on the Sabbath to do good or to do harm, to save life or to kill?" But they were silent. And he looked around at them with anger, grieved at their hardness of heart, and said to the man, "Stretch out your hand." He stretched it out, and his hand was restored.

> Mark 3:1-5

And he told his disciples to have a boat ready for him because of the crowd, lest they crush him, for he had healed many, so that all who had diseases pressed around him to touch him.

> Mark 3:9-10

And a great crowd followed him and thronged about him. And there was a woman who had had a discharge of blood for twelve years, and who had suffered much under many physicians, and had spent all that she had, and was no better but rather grew worse. She had heard the reports about Jesus and came up behind him in the crowd and touched his garment. For she said, "If I touch even his garments, I will be made well." And immediately the flow of blood dried up, and she felt in her body that she was healed of her disease. And Jesus, perceiving in himself that power had gone out from him, immediately turned about in the crowd and said, "Who touched my garments?" And his disciples said to him, "You see the crowd pressing around you, and yet you say, 'Who touched me?'" And he looked around to see who had done it. But the woman, knowing what had happened to her, came in fear and trembling and fell down before him and told him the whole truth. And he said to her, "Daughter, your faith has made you well; go in peace, and be healed of your disease."

Mark 5:24-34

And he could do no mighty work there, except that he laid his hands on a few sick people and healed them. And he marveled because of their unbelief.

Mark 6:5-6

And he called the twelve and began to send them out two by two, and gave them authority over the unclean spirits…So they went out and proclaimed that people should repent. And they cast out many demons and anointed with oil many who were sick and healed them.

Mark 6:7, 12-13

And wherever he came, in villages, cities, or countryside, they laid the sick in the marketplaces and implored him that they might touch even the fringe of his garment. And as many as touched it were made well.

Mark 6:56

And they brought to him a man who was deaf and had a speech impediment, and they begged him to lay his hand on him. And taking him aside from the crowd privately, he put his fingers into his ears, and after spitting touched his tongue. And looking up to heaven, he sighed and said to him, "Ephphatha," that is, "Be opened." And his ears were opened, his tongue was released, and he spoke plainly. And Jesus charged them to tell no one. But the more he charged them, the more zealously they proclaimed it. And they were astonished beyond measure, saying, "He has done all things well. He even makes the deaf hear and the mute speak."

Mark 7:32-37

And some people brought to him a blind man and begged him to touch him. And he took the blind man by the hand and led him out of the village, and when he had spit on his eyes and laid his hands on him, he asked him, "Do you see anything?" And he looked up and said, "I see people, but they look like trees, walking." Then Jesus laid his hands on his eyes again; and he opened his eyes, his sight was restored, and he saw everything clearly.

Mark 8:22-25

And as he was leaving Jericho with his disciples and a great crowd, Bartimaeus, a blind beggar, the son of Timaeus, was sitting by the roadside. And when he heard that it was Jesus of Nazareth, he began to cry out and say, "Jesus, Son of David, have mercy on me!" And many rebuked him, telling him to be silent. But he cried out all the more, "Son of David, have mercy on me!" And Jesus stopped and said, "Call him." And they called the blind man, saying to him, "Take heart. Get up; he is calling you." And throwing off his cloak, he sprang up and came to Jesus. And Jesus said to him, "What do you want me to do for you?" And the blind man said to him, "Rabbi, let me recover my sight." And Jesus said to him, "Go your way; your faith has made you well." And immediately he recovered his sight and followed him on the way.

Mark 10:46-52

Therefore I tell you, whatever you ask in prayer, believe that you have received it, and it will be yours.

Mark 11:24

And these signs will accompany those who believe: in my name they will cast out demons; they will speak in new tongues; they will pick up serpents with their hands; and if they drink any deadly poison, it will not hurt them; they will lay their hands on the sick, and they will recover."

Mark 16:17-18

And they went out and preached everywhere, while the Lord worked with them and confirmed the message by accompanying signs.

Mark 16:20

Healings

The Gospel According to
Luke

Now Simon's mother-in-law was ill with a high fever, and they appealed to him on her behalf. And he stood over her and rebuked the fever, and it left her, and immediately she rose and began to serve them.

Luke 4:38-39

Now when the sun was setting, all those who had any who were sick with various diseases brought them to him, and he laid his hands on every one of them and healed them.

Luke 4:40

While he was in one of the cities, there came a man full of leprosy. And when he saw Jesus, he fell on his face and begged him, "Lord, if you will, you can make me clean." And Jesus stretched out his hand and touched him, saying, "I will; be clean." And immediately the leprosy left him.

Luke 5:12-13

And behold, some men were bringing on a bed a man who was paralyzed, and they were seeking to bring him in and lay him before Jesus, but finding no way to bring him in, because of the crowd, they went up on the roof and let him down with his bed through the tiles into the midst before Jesus. And when he saw their faith, he said, "Man, your sins are forgiven you." And the scribes and the Pharisees began to question, saying, "Who is this who speaks blasphemies? Who can forgive sins but God alone?" When Jesus perceived their thoughts, he answered them, "Why do you question in your hearts? Which is easier, to say, 'Your sins are forgiven you,' or to say, 'Rise and walk'? But that you may know that the Son of Man has authority on earth to forgive sins"—he said to the man who was paralyzed— "I say to you, rise, pick up your bed and go home." And immediately he rose up before them and picked up what he had been lying on and went home, glorifying God.

> Luke 5:18-25

On another Sabbath, he entered the synagogue and was teaching, and a man was there whose right hand was withered. And the scribes and the Pharisees watched him, to see whether he would heal on the Sabbath, so that they might find a reason to accuse him. But he knew their thoughts, and he said to the man with the withered hand, "Come and stand here." And he rose and stood there. And Jesus said to them, "I ask you, is it lawful on the Sabbath to do good or to do harm, to save life or to destroy it?" And after looking around at them all he said to him, "Stretch out your hand." And he did so, and his hand was restored.

> Luke 6:6-10

And he came down with them and stood on a level place, with a great crowd of his disciples and a great multitude of people from all Judea and Jerusalem and the seacoast of Tyre and Sidon, who came to hear him and to be healed of their diseases. And those who were troubled with unclean spirits were cured. And all the crowd sought to touch him, for power came out from him and healed them all.

Luke 6:17-19

Now a centurion had a servant who was sick and at the point of death, who was highly valued by him. When the centurion heard about Jesus, he sent to him elders of the Jews, asking him to come and heal his servant...And Jesus went with them. When he was not far from the house, the centurion sent friends, saying to him, "Lord, do not trouble yourself, for I am not worthy to have you come under my roof. Therefore I did not presume to come to you. But say the word, and let my servant be healed...And when those who had been sent returned to the house, they found the servant well.

Luke 7:2-3, 6-7, 10

And he answered them, "Go and tell John what you have seen and heard: the blind receive their sight, the lame walk, lepers are cleansed, and the deaf hear, the dead are raised up, the poor have good news preached to them.

Luke 7:22

And the twelve were with him, and also some women who had been healed of evil spirits and infirmities: Mary, called Magdalene, from whom seven demons had gone out.

>	Luke 8:1-2

And there was a woman who had had a discharge of blood for twelve years, and though she had spent all her living on physicians, she could not be healed by anyone. She came up behind him and touched the fringe of his garment, and immediately her discharge of blood ceased. And Jesus said, "Who was it that touched me?" When all denied it, Peter said, "Master, the crowds surround you and are pressing in on you!" But Jesus said, "Someone touched me, for I perceive that power has gone out from me." And when the woman saw that she was not hidden, she came trembling, and falling down before him declared in the presence of all the people why she had touched him, and how she had been immediately healed. And he said to her, "Daughter, your faith has made you well; go in peace."

>	Luke 8:43-48

And he called the twelve together and gave them power and authority over all demons and to cure diseases, and he sent them out to proclaim the kingdom of God and to heal... And they departed and went through the villages, preaching the gospel and healing everywhere.

>	Luke 9:1-2, 6

When the crowds learned it, they followed him, and he welcomed them and spoke to them of the kingdom of God and cured those who had need of healing.

      Luke 9:11

Now he was casting out a demon that was mute. When the demon had gone out, the mute man spoke.

      Luke 11:14

And behold, there was a woman who had had a disabling spirit for eighteen years. She was bent over and could not fully straighten herself. When Jesus saw her, he called her over and said to her, "Woman, you are freed from your disability." And he laid his hands on her, and immediately she was made straight.

      Luke 13:11-13

And behold, there was a man before him who had dropsy. And Jesus responded to the lawyers and Pharisees, saying, "Is it lawful to heal on the Sabbath, or not?" But they remained silent. Then he took him and healed him and sent him away.

      Luke 14:2-4

And as he entered a village, he was met by ten lepers, who stood at a distance and lifted up their voices, saying, "Jesus, Master, have mercy on us." When he saw them he said to them, "Go and show yourselves to the priests." And as they went they were cleansed.

      Luke 17:12-14

As he drew near to Jericho, a blind man was sitting by the roadside begging. And hearing a crowd going by, he inquired what this meant. They told him, "Jesus of Nazareth is passing by." And he cried out, "Jesus, Son of David, have mercy on me!" And those who were in front rebuked him, telling him to be silent. But he cried out all the more, "Son of David, have mercy on me!" And Jesus stopped and commanded him to be brought to him. And when he came near, he asked him, "What do you want me to do for you?" He said, "Lord, let me recover my sight." And Jesus said to him, "Recover your sight; your faith has made you well." And immediately he recovered his sight.

      Luke 18:35-43

And when those who were around him saw what would follow, they said, "Lord, shall we strike with the sword?" And one of them struck the servant of the high priest and cut off his right ear. But Jesus said, "No more of this!" And he touched his ear and healed him.

      Luke 22:49-51

Healings

Gospel According to
John

And at Capernaum there was an official whose son was ill. When this man heard that Jesus had come from Judea to Galilee, he went to him and asked him to come down and heal his son, for he was at the point of death. So Jesus said to him, "Unless you see signs and wonders you will not believe." The official said to him, "Sir, come down before my child dies." Jesus said to him, "Go; your son will live." The man believed the word that Jesus spoke to him and went on his way. As he was going down, his servants met him and told him that his son was recovering. So he asked them the hour when he began to get better, and they said to him, "Yesterday at the seventh hour the fever left him." The father knew that was the hour when Jesus had said to him, "Your son will live."

John 4:46-53

One man was there who had been an invalid for thirty-eight years. When Jesus saw him lying there and knew that he had already been there a long time, he said to him, "Do you want to be healed?" The sick man answered him, "Sir, I have no one to put me into the pool when the water is stirred up, and while I am going another steps down before me." Jesus said to him, "Get up, take up your bed, and walk." And at once the man was healed, and he took up his bed and walked.

John 5:5-9

And a large crowd was following him, because they saw the signs that he was doing on the sick.

>John 6:2

Miracles

Gospel According to Matthew

And when he got into the boat, his disciples followed him. And behold, there arose a great storm on the sea, so that the boat was being swamped by the waves; but he was asleep. And they went and woke him, saying, "Save us, Lord; we are perishing." And he said to them, "Why are you afraid, O you of little faith?" Then he rose and rebuked the winds and the sea, and there was a great calm. And the men marveled, saying, "What sort of man is this, that even winds and sea obey him?"

Matthew 8:23-27

And when he came to the other side, to the country of the Gadarenes, two demon-possessed men met him, coming out of the tombs, so fierce that no one could pass that way. And behold, they cried out, "What have you to do with us, O Son of God? Have you come here to torment us before the time?" Now a herd of many pigs was feeding at some distance from them. And the demons begged him, saying, "If you cast us out, send us away into the herd of pigs." And he said to them, "Go." So they came out and went into the pigs, and behold, the whole herd rushed down the steep bank into the sea and drowned in the waters.

Matthew 8:28-32

While he was saying these things to them, behold, a ruler came in and knelt before him, saying, "My daughter has just died, but come and lay your hand on her, and she will live." And Jesus rose and followed him, with his disciples…And when Jesus came to the ruler's house and saw the flute players and the crowd making a commotion, he said, "Go away, for the girl is not dead but sleeping." And they laughed at him. But when the crowd had been put outside, he went in and took her by the hand, and the girl arose.

Matthew 9:18-19,23-25

As they were going away, behold, a demon-oppressed man who was mute was brought to him. And when the demon had been cast out, the mute man spoke.

Matthew 9:32-33

And he called to him his twelve disciples and gave them authority over unclean spirits, to cast them out, and to heal every disease and every affliction.

Matthew 10:1

And proclaim as you go, saying, 'The kingdom of heaven is at hand.' Heal the sick, raise the dead, cleanse lepers, cast out demons.

Matthew 10:7-8

Now when it was evening, the disciples came to him and said, "This is a desolate place, and the day is now over; send the crowds away to go into the villages and buy food for themselves." But Jesus said, "They need not go away; you give them something to eat." They said to him, "We have only five loaves here and two fish." And he said, "Bring them here to me." Then he ordered the crowds to sit down on the grass, and taking the five loaves and the two fish, he looked up to heaven and said a blessing. Then he broke the loaves and gave them to the disciples, and the disciples gave them to the crowds. And they all ate and were satisfied. And they took up twelve baskets full of the broken pieces left over. And those who ate were about five thousand men, besides women and children.

                                          Matthew 14:15-21

And after he had dismissed the crowds, he went up on the mountain by himself to pray. When evening came, he was there alone, but the boat by this time was a long way from the land, beaten by the waves, for the wind was against them. And in the fourth watch of the night he came to them, walking on the sea. But when the disciples saw him walking on the sea, they were terrified, and said, "It is a ghost!" and they cried out in fear. But immediately Jesus spoke to them, saying, "Take heart; it is I. Do not be afraid."

And Peter answered him, "Lord, if it is you, command me to come to you on the water." He said, "Come." So Peter got out of the boat and walked on the water and came to Jesus. But when he saw the wind, he was afraid, and beginning to sink he cried out, "Lord, save me." Jesus immediately reached out his hand and took hold of him, saying to him, "O you of little faith, why did you doubt?" And when they got into the boat, the wind ceased. And those in the boat worshiped him, saying, "Truly you are the Son of God."

Matthew 14:23-33

Then Jesus called his disciples to him and said, "I have compassion on the crowd because they have been with me now three days and have nothing to eat. And I am unwilling to send them away hungry, lest they faint on the way." And the disciples said to him, "Where are we to get enough bread in such a desolate place to feed so great a crowd?" And Jesus said to them, "How many loaves do you have?" They said, "Seven, and a few small fish." And directing the crowd to sit down on the ground, he took the seven loaves and the fish, and having given thanks he broke them and gave them to the disciples, and the disciples gave them to the crowds. And they all ate and were satisfied. And they took up seven baskets full of the broken pieces left over. Those who ate were four thousand men, besides women and children

Matthew 15:32-38

And when they came to the crowd, a man came up to him and, kneeling before him, said, "Lord, have mercy on my son, for he is an epileptic and he suffers terribly. For often he falls into the fire, and often into the water. And I brought him to your disciples, and they could not heal him." And Jesus answered, "O faithless and twisted generation, how long am I to be with you? How long am I to bear with you? Bring him here to me." And Jesus rebuked the demon, and it came out of him, and the boy was healed instantly. Then the disciples came to Jesus privately and said, "Why could we not cast it out?" He said to them, "Because of your little faith. For truly, I say to you, if you have faith like a grain of mustard seed, you will say to this mountain, 'Move from here to there,' and it will move, and nothing will be impossible for you."

Matthew 17:14-21

Miracles

The Gospel According to
Mark

And immediately there was in their synagogue a man with an unclean spirit. And he cried out, "What have you to do with us, Jesus of Nazareth? Have you come to destroy us? I know who you are—the Holy One of God." But Jesus rebuked him, saying, "Be silent, and come out of him!" And the unclean spirit, convulsing him and crying out with a loud voice, came out of him.

Mark 1:23-26

And he went throughout all Galilee, preaching in their synagogues and casting out demons.

Mark 1:39

And when he returned to Capernaum after some days, it was reported that he was at home. And many were gathered together, so that there was no more room, not even at the door. And he was preaching the word to them. And they came, bringing to him a paralytic carried by four men. And when they could not get near him because of the crowd, they removed the roof above him, and when they had made an opening, they let down the bed on which the paralytic lay. And when Jesus saw their faith, he said to the paralytic, "Son, your sins are forgiven." Now some of the scribes were sitting there, questioning in their hearts, "Why does this man speak like that? He is blaspheming! Who can forgive sins but God alone?" And immediately Jesus, perceiving in his spirit that they thus questioned within themselves, said to them, "Why do you question these things in your hearts? Which is easier, to say to the paralytic, 'Your sins are forgiven,' or to say, 'Rise, take up your bed and walk?' But that you may know that the Son of Man has authority on earth to forgive sins" —he said to the paralytic— "I say to you, rise, pick up your bed, and go home." And he rose and immediately picked up his bed and went out before them all, so that they were all amazed and glorified God, saying, "We never saw anything like this!"

Mark 2:1-12

And he appointed twelve (whom he also named apostles) so that they might be with him and he might send them out to preach and have authority to cast out demons.

Mark 3:14-15

On that day, when evening had come, he said to them, "Let us go across to the other side." And leaving the crowd, they took him with them in the boat, just as he was. And other boats were with him. And a great windstorm arose, and the waves were breaking into the boat, so that the boat was already filling. But he was in the stern, asleep on the cushion. And they woke him and said to him, "Teacher, do you not care that we are perishing?" And he awoke and rebuked the wind and said to the sea, "Peace! Be still!" And the wind ceased, and there was a great calm. He said to them, "Why are you so afraid? Have you still no faith?" And they were filled with great fear and said to one another, "Who then is this, that even the wind and the sea obey him?"

> Mark 4:35-41

They came to the other side of the sea, to the country of the Gerasenes. And when Jesus had stepped out of the boat, immediately there met him out of the tombs a man with an unclean spirit. He lived among the tombs. And no one could bind him anymore, not even with a chain, for he had often been bound with shackles and chains, but he wrenched the chains apart, and he broke the shackles in pieces. No one had the strength to subdue him. Night and day among the tombs and on the mountains he was always crying out and cutting himself with stones. And when he saw Jesus from afar, he ran and fell down before him. And crying out with a loud voice, he said, "What have you to do with me, Jesus, Son of the Most High God? I adjure you by God, do not torment me." For he was saying to him, "Come out of the man, you unclean spirit!" And Jesus asked him, "What is your name?" He replied, "My name is Legion, for we are many." And he begged him earnestly not to send them out of the country. Now a great herd of pigs was feeding there on the hillside, and they begged him, saying, "Send us to the pigs; let us enter them." So he gave them permission. And the unclean spirits came out and entered the pigs; and the herd, numbering about two thousand, rushed down the steep bank into the sea and drowned in the sea.

Mark 5:1-13

Then came one of the rulers of the synagogue, Jairus by name, and seeing him, he fell at his feet and implored him earnestly, saying, "My little daughter is at the point of death. Come and lay your hands on her, so that she may be made well and live." And he went with him…There came from the ruler's house some who said, "Your daughter is dead. Why trouble the Teacher any further?" But overhearing what they said, Jesus said to the ruler of the synagogue, "Do not fear, only believe." And he allowed no one to follow him except Peter and James and John the brother of James. They came to the house of the ruler of the synagogue, and Jesus saw a commotion, people weeping and wailing loudly. And when he had entered, he said to them, "Why are you making a commotion and weeping? The child is not dead but sleeping." And they laughed at him. But he put them all outside and took the child's father and mother and those who were with him and went in where the child was. Taking her by the hand he said to her, "Talitha cumi," which means, "Little girl, I say to you, arise." And immediately the girl got up and began walking (for she was twelve years of age), and they were immediately overcome with amazement.

Mark 5:22-24, 35-42

And he called the twelve and began to send them out two by two, and gave them authority over the unclean spirits...So they went out and proclaimed that people should repent. And they cast out many demons and anointed with oil many who were sick and healed them.

Mark 6:7, 12-13

When he went ashore he saw a great crowd, and he had compassion on them, because they were like sheep without a shepherd. And he began to teach them many things. And when it grew late, his disciples came to him and said, "This is a desolate place, and the hour is now late. Send them away to go into the surrounding countryside and villages and buy themselves something to eat." But he answered them, "You give them something to eat." And they said to him, "Shall we go and buy two hundred denarii worth of bread and give it to them to eat?" And he said to them, "How many loaves do you have? Go and see." And when they had found out, they said, "Five, and two fish." Then he commanded them all to sit down in groups on the green grass. So they sat down in groups, by hundreds and by fifties. And taking the five loaves and the two fish he looked up to heaven and said a blessing and broke the loaves and gave them to the disciples to set before the people. And he divided the two fish among them all. And they all ate and were satisfied. And they took up twelve baskets full of broken pieces and of the fish. And those who ate the loaves were five thousand men.

Mark 6:34-44

Immediately he made his disciples get into the boat and go before him to the other side, to Bethsaida, while he dismissed the crowd. And after he had taken leave of them, he went up on the mountain to pray. And when evening came, the boat was out on the sea, and he was alone on the land. And he saw that they were making headway painfully, for the wind was against them. And about the fourth watch of the night he came to them, walking on the sea. He meant to pass by them, but when they saw him walking on the sea they thought it was a ghost, and cried out, for they all saw him and were terrified. But immediately he spoke to them and said, "Take heart; it is I. Do not be afraid." And he got into the boat with them, and the wind ceased.

       Mark 6:45-51

But immediately a woman whose little daughter had an unclean spirit heard of him and came and fell down at his feet. Now the woman was a Gentile, a Syrophoenician by birth. And she begged him to cast the demon out of her daughter. And he said to her, "Let the children be fed first, for it is not right to take the children's bread and throw it to the dogs." But she answered him, "Yes, Lord; yet even the dogs under the table eat the children's crumbs." And he said to her, "For this statement you may go your way; the demon has left your daughter." And she went home and found the child lying in bed and the demon gone.

       Mark 7:25-30

In those days, when again a great crowd had gathered, and they had nothing to eat, he called his disciples to him and said to them, "I have compassion on the crowd, because they have been with me now three days and have nothing to eat. And if I send them away hungry to their homes, they will faint on the way. And some of them have come from far away." And his disciples answered him, "How can one feed these people with bread here in this desolate place?" And he asked them, "How many loaves do you have?" They said, "Seven." And he directed the crowd to sit down on the ground. And he took the seven loaves, and having given thanks, he broke them and gave them to his disciples to set before the people; and they set them before the crowd. And they had a few small fish. And having blessed them, he said that these also should be set before them. And they ate and were satisfied. And they took up the broken pieces left over, seven baskets full. And there were about four thousand people.

Mark 8:1-9

"Are your hearts hardened? Having eyes do you not see, and having ears do you not hear? And do you not remember? When I broke the five loaves for the five thousand, how many baskets full of broken pieces did you take up?" They said to him, "Twelve." "And the seven for the four thousand, how many baskets full of broken pieces did you take up?" And they said to him, "Seven." And he said to them, "Do you not yet understand?"

Mark 8:17-21

And they brought the boy to him. And when the spirit saw him, immediately it convulsed the boy, and he fell on the ground and rolled about, foaming at the mouth. And Jesus asked his father, "How long has this been happening to him?" And he said, "From childhood. And it has often cast him into fire and into water, to destroy him. But if you can do anything, have compassion on us and help us." And Jesus said to him, "'If you can!' All things are possible for one who believes." Immediately the father of the child cried out and said, "I believe; help my unbelief!" And when Jesus saw that a crowd came running together, he rebuked the unclean spirit, saying to it, "You mute and deaf spirit, I command you, come out of him and never enter him again." And after crying out and convulsing him terribly, it came out, and the boy was like a corpse, so that most of them said, "He is dead." But Jesus took him by the hand and lifted him up, and he arose.

Mark 9:20-27

On the following day, when they came from Bethany, he was hungry. And seeing in the distance a fig tree in leaf, he went to see if he could find anything on it. When he came to it, he found nothing but leaves, for it was not the season for figs. And he said to it, "May no one ever eat fruit from you again." And his disciples heard it...As they passed by in the morning, they saw the fig tree withered away to its roots. And Peter remembered and said to him, "Rabbi, look! The fig tree that you cursed has withered." And Jesus answered them, "Have faith in God. Truly, I say to you, whoever says to this mountain, 'Be taken up and thrown into the sea,' and does not doubt in his heart, but believes that what he says will come to pass, it will be done for him.

Therefore I tell you, whatever you ask in prayer, believe that you have received it, and it will be yours.

Mark 11:12-14, 20-24

And he sent two of his disciples and said to them, "Go into the city, and a man carrying a jar of water will meet you. Follow him, and wherever he enters, say to the master of the house, 'The Teacher says, Where is my guest room, where I may eat the Passover with my disciples?' And he will show you a large upper room furnished and ready; there prepare for us." And the disciples set out and went to the city and found it just as he had told them, and they prepared the Passover.

Mark 14:13-16

"And these signs will accompany those who believe: in my name they will cast out demons; they will speak in new tongues; they will pick up serpents with their hands; and if they drink any deadly poison, it will not hurt them; they will lay their hands on the sick, and they will recover."

Mark 16:17-18

And they went out and preached everywhere, while the Lord worked with them and confirmed the message by accompanying signs.

Mark 16:20

Miracles

The Gospel According to
Luke

And they rose up and drove him out of the town and brought him to the brow of the hill on which their town was built, so that they could throw him down the cliff. But passing through their midst, he went away.

                                      Luke 4:29-30

And in the synagogue there was a man who had the spirit of an unclean demon, and he cried out with a loud voice, "Ha! What have you to do with us, Jesus of Nazareth? Have you come to destroy us? I know who you are —the Holy One of God." But Jesus rebuked him, saying, "Be silent and come out of him!" And when the demon had thrown him down in their midst, he came out of him, having done him no harm.

                                      Luke 4:33-35

And demons also came out of many, crying, "You are the Son of God!" But he rebuked them and would not allow them to speak.

                                      Luke 4:41

And when he had finished speaking, he said to Simon, "Put out into the deep and let down your nets for a catch." And Simon answered, "Master, we toiled all night and took nothing! But at your word I will let down the nets." And when they had done this, they enclosed a large number of fish, and their nets were breaking. They signaled to their partners in the other boat to come and help them. And they came and filled both the boats, so that they began to sink.

Luke 5:4-7

And he answered them, "Go and tell John what you have seen and heard: the blind receive their sight, the lame walk, lepers are cleansed, and the deaf hear, the dead are raised up, the poor have good news preached to them.

Luke 7:22

And the twelve were with him, and also some women who had been healed of evil spirits and infirmities: Mary, called Magdalene, from whom seven demons had gone out.

Luke 8:1-2

And as they sailed he fell asleep. And a windstorm came down on the lake, and they were filling with water and were in danger. And they went and woke him, saying, "Master, Master, we are perishing!" And he awoke and rebuked the wind and the raging waves, and they ceased, and there was a calm.

Luke 8:23-24

When Jesus had stepped out on land, there met him a man from the city who had demons. For a long time he had worn no clothes, and he had not lived in a house but among the tombs. When he saw Jesus, he cried out and fell down before him and said with a loud voice, "What have you to do with me, Jesus, Son of the Most High God? I beg you, do not torment me." For he had commanded the unclean spirit to come out of the man. (For many a time it had seized him. He was kept under guard and bound with chains and shackles, but he would break the bonds and be driven by the demon into the desert.) Jesus then asked him, "What is your name?" And he said, "Legion," for many demons had entered him. And they begged him not to command them to depart into the abyss. Now a large herd of pigs was feeding there on the hillside, and they begged him to let them enter these. So he gave them permission. Then the demons came out of the man and entered the pigs, and the herd rushed down the steep bank into the lake and drowned.

Luke 8:27-33

And there came a man named Jairus, who was a ruler of the synagogue. And falling at Jesus' feet, he implored him to come to his house for he had an only daughter, about twelve years of age, and she was dying...While he was still speaking, someone from the ruler's house came and said, "Your daughter is dead; do not trouble the Teacher any more." But Jesus on hearing this answered him, "Do not fear; only believe, and she will be well." And when he came to the house, he allowed no one to enter with him, except Peter and John and James, and the father and mother of the child. And all were weeping and mourning for her, but he said, "Do not weep, for she is not dead but sleeping." And they laughed at him, knowing that she was dead. But taking her by the hand he called, saying, "Child, arise." And her spirit returned, and she got up at once. And he directed that something should be given her to eat.

Luke 8:41-42, 49-55

And he called the twelve together and gave them power and authority over all demons and to cure diseases, and he sent them out to proclaim the kingdom of God and to heal.

Luke 9:1-2

Now the day began to wear away, and the twelve came and said to him, "Send the crowd away to go into the surrounding villages and countryside to find lodging and get provisions, for we are here in a desolate place." But he said to them, "You give them something to eat." They said, "We have no more than five loaves and two fish —unless we are to go and buy food for all these people." For there were about five thousand men. And he said to his disciples, "Have them sit down in groups of about fifty each." And they did so, and had them all sit down. And taking the five loaves and the two fish, he looked up to heaven and said a blessing over them. Then he broke the loaves and gave them to the disciples to set before the crowd. And they all ate and were satisfied. And what was left over was picked up, twelve baskets of broken pieces.

Luke 9:12-17

Now about eight days after these sayings he took with him Peter and John and James and went up on the mountain to pray. And as he was praying, the appearance of his face was altered, and his clothing became dazzling white. And behold, two men were talking with him, Moses and Elijah, who appeared in glory and spoke of his departure, which he was about to accomplish at Jerusalem. Now Peter and those who were with him were heavy with sleep, but when they became fully awake they saw his glory and the two men who stood with him. And as the men were parting from him, Peter said to Jesus, "Master, it is good that we are here. Let us make three tents, one for you and one for Moses and one for Elijah"—not knowing what he said. As he was saying these things, a cloud came and overshadowed them, and they were afraid as they entered the cloud. And a voice came out of the cloud, saying, "This is my Son, my Chosen One; listen to him!" And when the voice had spoken, Jesus was found alone.

Luke 9:28-36

And behold, a man from the crowd cried out, "Teacher, I beg you to look at my son, for he is my only child. And behold, a spirit seizes him, and he suddenly cries out. It convulses him so that he foams at the mouth, and shatters him, and will hardly leave him…" While he was coming, the demon threw him to the ground and convulsed him. But Jesus rebuked the unclean spirit and healed the boy, and gave him back to his father.

Luke 9:38-39, 42

The seventy-two returned with joy, saying, "Lord, even the demons are subject to us in your name!" And he said to them, "I saw Satan fall like lightning from heaven. Behold, I have given you authority to tread on serpents and scorpions, and over all the power of the enemy, and nothing shall hurt you.

> Luke 10:17-19

Now he was casting out a demon that was mute. When the demon had gone out, the mute man spoke.

> Luke 11:14

"Behold, I cast out demons and perform cures today and tomorrow."

> Luke 13:32

Miracles

The Gospel According to
John

Now there were six stone water jars there for the Jewish rites of purification, each holding twenty or thirty gallons. Jesus said to the servants, "Fill the jars with water." And they filled them up to the brim. And he said to them, "Now draw some out and take it to the master of the feast." So they took it. When the master of the feast tasted the water now become wine, and did not know where it came from (though the servants who had drawn the water knew), the master of the feast called the bridegroom and said to him, "Everyone serves the good wine first, and when people have drunk freely, then the poor wine. But you have kept the good wine until now." This, the first of his signs, Jesus did at Cana in Galilee, and manifested his glory.

John 2:6-11

This man came to Jesus by night and said to him, "Rabbi, we know that you are a teacher come from God, for no one can do these signs that you do unless God is with him."

John 3:2

The woman answered him, "I have no husband." Jesus said to her, "You are right in saying, 'I have no husband;' for you have had five husbands, and the one you now have is not your husband. What you have said is true." The woman said to him, "Sir, I perceive that you are a prophet."

John 4:17-19

For the Father loves the Son and shows him all that he himself is doing. And greater works than these will he show him, so that you may marvel. For as the Father raises the dead and gives them life, so also the Son gives life to whom he will.

John 5:20-21

Lifting up his eyes, then, and seeing that a large crowd was coming toward him, Jesus said to Philip, "Where are we to buy bread, so that these people may eat?" He said this to test him, for he himself knew what he would do. Philip answered him, "Two hundred denarii worth of bread would not be enough for each of them to get a little." One of his disciples, Andrew, Simon Peter's brother, said to him, "There is a boy here who has five barley loaves and two fish, but what are they for so many?" Jesus said, "Have the people sit down." Now there was much grass in the place. So the men sat down, about five thousand in number. Jesus then took the loaves, and when he had given thanks, he distributed them to those who were seated. So also the fish, as much as they wanted. And when they had eaten their fill, he told his disciples, "Gather up the leftover fragments, that nothing may be lost."

So they gathered them up and filled twelve baskets with fragments from the five barley loaves left by those who had eaten.

John 6:5-13

It was now dark, and Jesus had not yet come to them. The sea became rough because a strong wind was blowing. When they had rowed about three or four miles, they saw Jesus walking on the sea and coming near the boat, and they were frightened. But he said to them, "It is I; do not be afraid." Then they were glad to take him into the boat, and immediately the boat was at the land to which they were going.

John 6:17-21

As he passed by, he saw a man blind from birth. And his disciples asked him, "Rabbi, who sinned, this man or his parents, that he was born blind?" Jesus answered, "It was not that this man sinned, or his parents, but that the works of God might be displayed in him. We must work the works of him who sent me while it is day; night is coming, when no one can work. As long as I am in the world, I am the light of the world." Having said these things, he spit on the ground and made mud with the saliva. Then he anointed the man's eyes with the mud and said to him, "Go, wash in the pool of Siloam" (which means Sent). So he went and washed and came back seeing.

John 9:1-7

Then Jesus, deeply moved again, came to the tomb. It was a cave, and a stone lay against it. Jesus said, "Take away the stone." Martha, the sister of the dead man, said to him, "Lord, by this time there will be an odor, for he has been dead four days." Jesus said to her, "Did I not tell you that if you believed you would see the glory of God?" So they took away the stone. And Jesus lifted up his eyes and said, "Father, I thank you that you have heard me. I knew that you always hear me, but I said this on account of the people standing around, that they may believe that you sent me." When he had said these things, he cried out with a loud voice, "Lazarus, come out." The man who had died came out, his hands and feet bound with linen strips, and his face wrapped with a cloth. Jesus said to them, "Unbind him, and let him go."

John 11:38-44

Just as day was breaking, Jesus stood on the shore; yet the disciples did not know that it was Jesus. Jesus said to them, "Children, do you have any fish?" They answered him, "No." He said to them, "Cast the net on the right side of the boat, and you will find some." So they cast it, and now they were not able to haul it in, because of the quantity of fish.

John 21:4-6

Want more of Marjorie Lou?

Get your free eBook today!

KingdomPurposeLife.com/free-ebook-power-kingdom

Do you know how God uses His power?
The answer will surprise you!

Be encouraged in the Word!

Join a community of Believers!

See the latest posts, audios and testimonies!

Just a click away!

KingdomPurposeLife.com
KingdomPurposeWomen.com

Facebook Pages: @kingdompurposelife
@kingdompurposewomen

Twitter: @marjorie_lou_

Invite Marjorie Lou to speak at your

- Conference
- Seminar
- Church
- Event

Learn more at

MarjorieLou.com

Facebook: @marjorielouministries

See a full list of resources from
Marjorie Lou
and Marjorie Lou Ministries

MarjorieLou.com

Facebook: @marjorielouministries
Twitter: @Marjorie_Lou_

www.ingramcontent.com/pod-product-compliance
Lightning Source LLC
Chambersburg PA
CBHW060839050426
42453CB00008B/758